The Cherokee

A Proud People

Suzanne Cloud Tapper

Enslow Elementary
an imprint of
Enslow Publishers, Inc.

40 Industrial Road   PO Box 38
Box 398   Aldershot
Berkeley Heights, NJ 07922   Hants GU12 6BP
USA   UK

http://www.enslow.com

Editor's Note: *The people of this book called themselves Aniyunwiya or Yunwiya, meaning "Principal People." During ceremonial events, they would call themselves Keetoowah. "Cherokee" is a word that another American Indian nation had for the Aniyunwiya. When they came to the Aniyunwiya lands, White American settlers began using the name Cherokee for the Aniyunwiya people. Today, the Aniyunwiya have come to call themselves the Cherokee, or Tsalagi in their language. For this reason, we at Enslow Publishers, Inc., have used the word "Cherokee" when referring to them.*

Enslow Elementary, an imprint of Enslow Publishers, Inc.

Enslow Elementary ® is a registered trademark of Enslow Publishers, Inc.

Library of Congress Cataloging-in-Publication Data

Cloud Tapper, Suzanne.
    The Cherokee : a proud people / Suzanne Cloud Tapper.
      p. cm. — (American Indians) (Includes bibliographical references and index.)
    ISBN 0-7660-2454-7
    1. Cherokee Indians—History—Juvenile literature. 2. Cherokee Indians—Social life and customs—Juvenile literature. I. Title. II. Series. III. American Indians (Berkeley Heights, N.J.)
E99.C5C666 2005
975.004'97557—dc22

2004016149

Printed in the United States of America

10 9 8 7 6 5 4 3 2 1

To Our Readers: We have done our best to make sure all Internet addresses in this book were active and appropriate when we went to press. However, the author and the publisher have no control over and assume no liability for the material available on those Internet sites or on other Web sites they may link to. Any comments or suggestions can be sent by e-mail to comments@enslow.com or to the address on the back cover.

Illustration Credits: Associated Press, AP, p. 41; Clipart.com, p. 39; Denver Public Library, Western History Collection, p. 47; Department of Defense, pp. 1 (right), 28; © Corel Corporation, pp. 14 (bottom), 29; Enslow Publishers, Inc., p. 7; © Marilyn "Angel" Wynn/Nativestock.com, pp. 1 (left, middle, and background), 4, 6, 8, 9, 12, 13, 15, 16, 17, 18, 19, 20, 21, 22, 23, 24, 25, 26, 30, 31, 34, 35, 36, 37, 43, 44; Photos.com, pp. 14 (top), 27; Tommy Wildcat, p. 33; Reproduced from the Collections of the Library of Congress, pp. 38, 42; Reproduced from the Dictionary of American Portraits, published by Dover Publications, Inc., in 1967, p. 40; © Topham/The Image Works, p. 32.

Front Cover: Department of Defense (right); © Marilyn "Angel" Wynn/Nativestock.com (left, middle, and background)

Back Cover: Denver Public Library, Western History Collection

Contents

This Cherokee hoop dancer celebrates at one of his nation's many powwows.

The Principal People

Recently, a Cherokee Nation council member was preparing to go to fight in Iraq. Soldier Shawnna Eubanks said, "I have two kids . . . I know I will miss them." Her friend John Ketcher proudly said, "Cherokee people are the most patriotic people in the U.S."

Cherokee pride is rooted in a way of life that goes back at least thirteen hundred years. Before the Europeans came, the Cherokee were a part of a great American Indian group that historians call the Mississippian Culture Complex. These ancient American Indians built mounds that are still present today. The Cherokee then split away from this group and developed their own ways. They called themselves Aniyunwiya or Yunwiya, meaning "the Principal People" because they believed they were the center of the world.

chapter one

The Land

In the Southeast, a group of American Indians built large mounds of earth. This group of people lasted from about 3000 B.C. to A.D. 1539. The Cherokee are descendants of these mound builders. They came to live in the hills and mountains of the southern Appalachian Mountains.

The Cherokee Then

The Cherokee spread out into North Carolina, South Carolina, eastern Tennessee, Alabama, and northern Georgia. In 1838, most Cherokee were forced out of their homes and made to

The Cherokee developed from a civilization of mound builders.

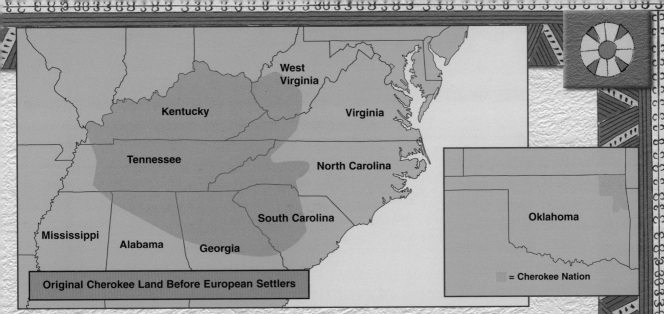

The original land of the Cherokee covered most of the present-day southeastern United States. The land of the Cherokee Nation now covers nearly fourteen counties in Oklahoma (inset).

march west to Indian Territory (now Oklahoma). Some white Americans of the Southeast wanted Cherokee land, and powerful people in the government agreed. The Cherokee name for the march was "the trail where we cried." In English, it was called the Trail of Tears.

The Cherokee Today

Now, the Cherokee are divided into three groups: the Cherokee Nation in Oklahoma; the United Keetoowah Band of Cherokee Indians in Oklahoma; and those who remained in the mountains of North Carolina, called the Eastern Band of Cherokee Indians.

chapter two

History

In 1540, Spanish explorer Hernando de Soto came to what would become the United States. He was searching for gold. De Soto and his men were the first Europeans seen by the Cherokee. However, the Europeans brought many diseases that the American Indians had no protection against. Many of the American Indians died.

In the mid-1600s, two English traders came to the Cherokee town of Chota. They traded for deerskin, beeswax, and bear fat. Once again, the Cherokee were amazed to see Europeans.

At times, the Cherokee fought to protect their territory

This model of a Cherokee village shows both summer (middle) and winter homes (left), a meeting house (top right), and a garden (bottom).

from the colonists. In the Revolutionary War, they joined the British to fight the American colonists.

In 1791, the United States wanted the Cherokee to stop hunting and start farming. They promised that, if the Cherokee did so, they could keep their land. An agreement was made. Cherokee Chief Bloody Fellow told an American official, "The treaty mentions ploughs, hoes, cattle, and other things for a farm; this is what we want; game is going fast away among us. We must plant corn and raise cattle . . . we desire you to assist us."

In the early 1800s, the Cherokee invented a syllabary (much like an alphabet), wrote laws, and started a newspaper. However, gold was discovered and white Americans wanted Cherokee land. President Andrew Jackson decided that all the American Indians living there had to be moved from their homeland. In 1838, the

United States forced almost all of the Cherokee to march many miles. Thousands died from lack of food and sickness. The walk was called the Trail of Tears.

In the late 1800s, the Cherokee Nation of Oklahoma rebuilt their nation. They started schools to make sure their heritage would not disappear. They formed the Cherokee Historical Society, which now gets 2.5 million visitors a year.

In 1987, the first woman chief, Wilma Mankiller, was

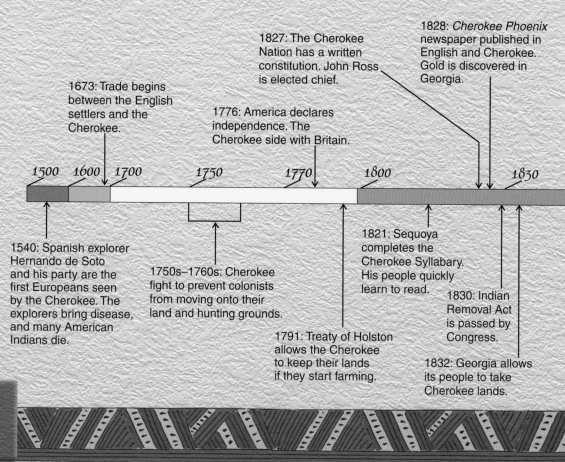

1827: The Cherokee Nation has a written constitution. John Ross is elected chief.

1828: *Cherokee Phoenix* newspaper published in English and Cherokee. Gold is discovered in Georgia.

1673: Trade begins between the English settlers and the Cherokee.

1776: America declares independence. The Cherokee side with Britain.

1500   1600   1700   1750   1770   1800   1830

1540: Spanish explorer Hernando de Soto and his party are the first Europeans seen by the Cherokee. The explorers bring disease, and many American Indians die.

1750s–1760s: Cherokee fight to prevent colonists from moving onto their land and hunting grounds.

1791: Treaty of Holston allows the Cherokee to keep their lands if they start farming.

1821: Sequoya completes the Cherokee Syllabary. His people quickly learn to read.

1830: Indian Removal Act is passed by Congress.

1832: Georgia allows its people to take Cherokee lands.

elected to lead the Cherokee Nation. The Western Cherokee Nation and the Eastern Cherokee finally met together in 1984 in Red Clay, Tennessee. They agreed to work together to protect the Cherokee way of life. A group of Cherokee Nation members serving in Iraq are now planning to bring some American Indian culture to the Middle East. Three soldiers that are living in Iraq are organizing what is believed to be the first powwow ever held in that country.

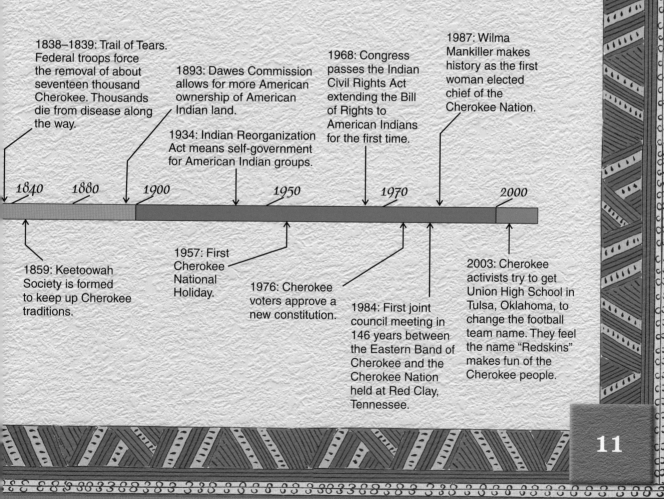

1838–1839: Trail of Tears. Federal troops force the removal of about seventeen thousand Cherokee. Thousands die from disease along the way.

1893: Dawes Commission allows for more American ownership of American Indian land.

1934: Indian Reorganization Act means self-government for American Indian groups.

1968: Congress passes the Indian Civil Rights Act extending the Bill of Rights to American Indians for the first time.

1987: Wilma Mankiller makes history as the first woman elected chief of the Cherokee Nation.

1840   1880   1900   1950   1970   2000

1859: Keetoowah Society is formed to keep up Cherokee traditions.

1957: First Cherokee National Holiday.

1976: Cherokee voters approve a new constitution.

1984: First joint council meeting in 146 years between the Eastern Band of Cherokee and the Cherokee Nation held at Red Clay, Tennessee.

2003: Cherokee activists try to get Union High School in Tulsa, Oklahoma, to change the football team name. They feel the name "Redskins" makes fun of the Cherokee people.

chapter three

Homes

Whether today or in the past, the Cherokee have always looked for a place to live in peace.

The Cherokee Then

Each Cherokee village had a large town house. The house had seven sides, one for every clan (group of families), and each Cherokee would sit by his or her clan. The walls were made from young tree branches covered with dried mud. Benches lined the walls and a fire was in

The large round house was used for meetings and ceremonies.

This is the type of house that most Cherokee lived in before the Europeans came.

After the Cherokee began to trade with the Europeans, their homes began to look different inside.

Fires kept the Cherokee warm on cold nights.

the middle. This is where the town council would meet to discuss tribal business. There were no windows, just a small door opening onto a large plaza. The plaza is where the town ceremonies and dances were held.

Private homes surrounded the town house. They were large enough for grandparents, parents, and children to live together. In summer, they lived in large rectangular houses. In winter, they lived in small round houses called osi. These were dark and smoky because

The Cherokee first lived in the American southwest. It was important for them to live near a source of water, like the Bald River in Tennessee.

a fire was kept burning in the center for warmth. Outside, each house had a small garden. The Cherokee always had a pot of stew or soup on the fire for hungry guests.

The Cherokee Today

Today, the Cherokee people live in houses that are built much like those of other Americans. However, they still have their central council chamber to talk about tribal problems. They also still hold their special ceremonies in open plazas.

This Cherokee Nation Council House looks like a typical modern American home.

chapter four

Clothing

When Europeans first arrived, the Cherokee children wore nothing. In winter, men and women wore deerskin cloaks with moccasins laced up the legs.

The Cherokee Then

The Cherokee "tear dress" was a favorite of women. The "ribbon shirt" was common for men. The tear dress came from the Trail of Tears era. Many of the women had no scissors. Most of the Cherokee were not prepared for the long march. So material was torn to make pieces to sew together. The skirt length was shortened to keep the ground from soiling it. Sleeves were

This coat was worn by a Cherokee chief in the winter. It is made from turkey feathers.

shorter, too, to make it easy for women to grind corn and wash dishes.

Cherokee women stitched many patterns onto their clothing. Triangles, circles, and even the seven-sided star of the Cherokee were used. The ribbon shirt had ribbons on the front and back.

The Cherokee Today

Today, both the tear dress and ribbon shirt are mostly worn for ceremonial purposes. Women's tear dresses are not as short as they used to be. Only Cherokee wear the tear dress, but men from other American Indian groups have worn the ribbon shirt, especially at powwows. Today, the tear dresses reach the floor. The everyday clothes the Cherokee wear today are the same kinds of clothes that most other Americans wear.

The Cherokee men in this picture are wearing ribbon shirts. The women wear tear dresses.

chapter five

Food and Meals

The Cherokee used to hunt often. After the white American settlers came, the Cherokee farmed more than they hunted.

The Cherokee Then

The men caught meat for the family, and hunting trips could last several months. Cherokee custom was to call all of the neighbors together to share the deer and turkey.

Cherokee grew their own food. The men cleared the fields. The women put seeds in the ground. Both helped with the harvest. Most of the food was grown in large fields that the women worked together. Crops were corn, beans, sunflowers, and pumpkins. In fact, corn was used in almost everything—soups, stews, and bread. Corn was so important that, when it was ready to eat every year, the Green Corn Ceremony

Cherokee men hunted and trapped animals for food. This animal trap was built from a type of plant called river cane.

This couple performs the Green Corn Dance.

was held. For four days in late June, the Cherokee would celebrate with stomp dances and fasting (not eating for a certain amount of time), then feasting and prayer.

The Cherokee Today

Traditional Cherokee dishes are bean bread, fried hominy, and grape dumplings. A Cherokee treat still made today is *kanuchi*. It is prepared in a hollowed-out log. Dried hickory nuts are shelled and placed in the log. The nuts are pounded until they can be formed into balls, then simmered in water until the mixture is thick. The Cherokee then added some dried corn and sugar and served it hot.

The Cherokee eat corn and squash. They also eat acorn bread, hominy grits, and mustard greens (on plate).

chapter six

Marriage and Family

Every Cherokee is a member of a clan. A clan is a group of families. The Cherokee have seven clans: Wolf, Deer, Bird, Paint, Long Hair, Blue, and Wild Potato.

The Cherokee Then

The mother is the head of the family. In the past, the family lived in the house of the mother. A woman cannot marry a man from her own clan or her father's clan. If a woman from the Deer Clan married a man from the Bird Clan, their children would be members of the Deer Clan. However, the father remains a member of

In this 1909 photo, a father transports his children on a device called a "travois" that is pulled by a horse.

This Cherokee mother is proud of her child, who has just won a trophy at a local fair.

the Bird Clan. The children are raised and protected by their mother's brother.

During the traditional Cherokee wedding ceremony, the bride's brother and mother stood with her. The brother took a vow to teach her children well. He would take the role of uncle, or e-du-tsi. The bride and groom then met near the sacred fire in the town house. A priest or priestess would bless them. Songs were sung. The bride and groom were then each covered in a blue blanket. At the right moment, these blankets would be removed and replaced with one white blanket. The groom gave the bride a piece of deer meat. She gave him an ear of corn. This meant that he would keep the family well fed and she would be a good wife. Then the people celebrated.

The Cherokee Today

Cherokee still use some of these traditions. However, they also have weddings that are similar to other Americans.

chapter seven

Everyday Life of Children

The days of Cherokee children were filled with important lessons. In the past, they were taught outside in the fields, gardens, and woods. Today, they are taught in schools.

The Cherokee Then

In the late 1700s, a typical day in the life of a young Cherokee girl or boy was very different. Young children might start the day eating a breakfast of bean bread and fried squirrel with their mother and father. However, they would then go their separate ways.

A young boy would be trained by his uncles. They

A Cherokee boy kept his arrows in a quiver. He would learn from his uncles how to hunt bear.

would teach him how to make weapons and how to hunt deer and bear. He would also study the art of carving stone and wood.

A young Cherokee girl would spend the day helping her mother. She would learn to cook meals for the family over the house fire. She was taught how to plant corn, squash, and other vegetables in the fields around the village. A Cherokee girl would spend her day making clothing from deerskin for herself or for her brothers. She might spend some time taking care of the youngest children while her mother worked in the garden. A Cherokee girl might also spend the afternoon collecting wild fruit like strawberries to share at dinner.

Cherokee children were always treated with respect.

The art of wood carving takes great concentration.

No one was allowed to ever hit or spank a Cherokee child. If a child had to be corrected, elders would lightly make fun of him or her. That was all the discipline that was needed in order to get the child to behave.

This Cherokee competes in a bow and arrow contest at a local fair. Many Cherokee are taught how to use the bow and arrow when they are children.

At dinner, the family would gather to eat a meal of roasted rabbit or wild onions and eggs. If visitors dropped by, they would be asked to join the family. Cherokee hospitality is famous. After dinner, friends and family would tell stories. Stories about animals were favorites. Stories about past family members, places, and how things came to be were told over and over again. The Cherokee did not have schools then, so they told stories to teach their children about life.

The Cherokee Today

Cherokee children attend school rather than hunt or plant seeds. However, modern Cherokee children are taught about their history and culture. If they want to hear stories like "How the Possum Lost His Tail" or "The Story of the Bat," there is always someone to tell the tale. Sometimes, they even attend powwows, where there is dancing and many other activities.

Cherokee children play on a playground on a reservation in North Carolina.

chapter eight

Religion and Medicine

The Cherokee feel that their survival comes from their closeness to the land.

The Cherokee Then

The Cherokee gain strength from their faithfulness to Duyukta. This means "the right way" or "the path of being in balance." Animals, plants, and other natural events play important parts in Cherokee stories. The Cherokee religion says human beings and animals are the same. Like humans,

This statue of a medicine man, or shaman, shows him holding up an offering in a stone pottery vessel.

the animals belong to groups with chiefs, town houses, and councils. All rivers are called "Long Man" and are sacred.

Dances and songs came from the killing of a monster called Stone Coat. He was named that because his skin was solid rock. As Stone Coat burned in the fire, he began singing songs. These songs were gifts to the Cherokee. They were learned and passed on to the young. The songs were sung in ceremonies and before a hunt. They were also sung for victory in warfare and as medicine to cure sickness.

Tea made from blackberries was used by the Cherokee for stomach aches.

Cherokee medicine people used common herbs, flowers, and berries to cure illnesses. Tea made from blackberries soothed the stomach. Mint was used for itchy skin. Willow bark was dried, made into tea, and used for aches and pains. Persimmon was used for earaches.

The Cherokee Today

Today, the Cherokee blend ancient beliefs with other religions. Because missionaries spent years with the Cherokee in the 1800s, many of them became Christians. Some Cherokee celebrate their old traditions and mix them with new ones. For example, in December, they may

A Cherokee children's choir performs at the opening of the National Museum of the American Indian in Washington, D.C.

celebrate Christmas; and, in late June or early July, they would celebrate the Green Corn Ceremony.

The Cherokee also blend traditional medicine with the medicine of today. Ken Masters, a Cherokee artist, told about his grandfather using persimmons on him when he was a little boy. "He put a small drop [of persimmon juice] into my hurting ear. In just a little while . . . I went to sleep with

The black-eyed Susan flower can help stop pain from an insect bite.

no earache. I never had another one." Many Cherokee still use the black-eyed Susan flower to ease the pain of an insect bite, but they also take children to the doctor for regular check-ups.

Arts and Music

Art and music are an important part of Cherokee life.

The Cherokee Then

There were many Cherokee musical instruments. One was the water drum, a hollowed-out log with water placed in it. A deerskin was stretched over the top.

The river cane flute was about one foot long and had five or six holes. It had a very calm and haunting sound.

Tapping sticks were also made out of river cane.

This Cherokee grass skirt dancer performs at a powwow. All types of musical instruments combine to create beautiful Cherokee music.

Though this clay vessel and basket were used for cooking and storing food, they are considered works of art today.

Cherokee musicians held one in each hand and tapped them together.

Gourds were used to make shakers. Small stones or clay beads were put inside. Clay whistles were made in the shape of a frog or bird and made a high-pitched sound when they were blown.

The Cherokee also carved bone, stone, and wood into beautiful art. They would trade with other tribes for seashells. Then, they carved breastplates from conch and clamshells. Earrings were made from scallop shells. Necklaces were made of carved bone and wooden beads. Some Cherokee artists would carve clan animal figures on ceremonial pipes.

Cherokee women made baskets from river cane, white oak, hickory bark, and honeysuckle. They would dye them with black walnut and bloodroot. Baskets were needed in early Cherokee house. Different types of food was gathered and stored in them. Some baskets were even made waterproof so that they could be used to hold water and for cooking.

This bandolier bag is decorated with beautiful designs. It would have been worn across a Cherokee man's chest.

The Cherokee Today

Today, Cherokee musicians make their own drums and flutes. They perform all over the world. Tommy Wildcat is known as one of the finest Cherokee flutists. Turtle-shell rattles are still used in ceremonies. Men hold a single rattle in their hands

Tommy Wildcat stands in the forest with his flute. Wildcat is one of the best Cherokee flutists.

and women wear them tied to their legs as they dance.

The Cherokee often tell stories about their music, which is a very powerful force in their lives. "My great-grandfather would get up in the morning and the first thing he would do in the morning was face east and sing a song. It was a greeting to the sun. Art is life and life is art. Song is prayer," said Ken Masters.

The Cherokee continue to make baskets as well as pottery. As the years have gone by, Cherokee art has become more colorful and intricate.

chapter ten

Sports and Games

The Cherokee played a game much like lacrosse.

The Cherokee Then

Stickball was a very rough game. It was played like modern lacrosse. Two teams used netted sticks to catch and throw the ball. The ball was made from deer hide.

At the start of the game, the ball was tossed into the air by a shaman. The players were only the best male athletes. When a player hit a wooden fish on the top of a pole with the ball, seven points were scored for his team.

Chunkey was a game enjoyed by almost all of the

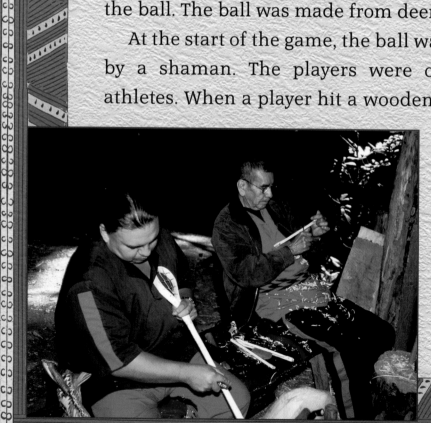

Two Cherokee carve stickball sticks from hickory wood.

These women play stickball in a tournament at the Annual Cherokee Indian Fair in North Carolina.

Southeastern Indians. This game was usually played by two players. One would start a smooth stone disk rolling on the ground. Then both players would try to hit the moving stone with eight-foot poles. The people watching would bet on whose pole would be closest to the stone when it stopped rolling. This game would be played all day.

The Cherokee Today

Stickball is an important part of modern Cherokee activities at their Stomp Grounds. The Stomp Grounds are the central focal point of all ceremonies. The Cherokee still use the original square shape for the area. Today, women also play stickball.

chapter eleven

Warfare

The Cherokee of the Southeast made war against other nearby American Indians and colonists who disrespected Cherokee land. Land was sacred to the Cherokee, and people had to be invited to be accepted. The land was important because they hunted there.

The Cherokee Then

War was also a way to avenge the killing of relatives. Sometimes, war captives were adopted as family members. Those adopted enjoyed full rights as members of the community if they were seen as worthy.

Common weapons were spears, tomahawks, blow guns, and bows and arrows. Raiding other tribal villages was a

This weapon was used as a war club and as an ax.

Blow guns and darts were sometimes made from river cane. Today, some southeastern Cherokee still have blow gun contests.

way for the Cherokee to get needed food and livestock. Going to war was very important for young Cherokee men. Warriors gained status through war.

In the early 1700s, American colonists urged the Cherokee Indians to make peace with the Tuscarora Indians. The Cherokee explained that their enemy was a needed and worthy opponent. The threat of the Tuscarora was important for young Cherokee teens who needed battle experience.

The Cherokee Today

The Cherokee have fought in many of America's modern wars. In 2004, the Cherokee began raising funds for the Cherokee Nation Warriors Memorial by selling "honor bricks" for twenty-five dollars. Each brick honors a Cherokee veteran from an American war.

chapter twelve

Heroes

Cherokee heroes have taken many different forms.

The Cherokee Then

One of the greatest Cherokee heroes was Sequoyah. He never learned to speak or write English. However, he was curious about how Europeans and Americans "talked" by making marks on paper. Sequoyah began to make his own system of writing. He thought of a mark for every syllable in the Cherokee language. (A syllable is part of a word.

Sequoyah invented the Cherokee Syllabary. Because of Sequoyah's invention, his people were able to write their language, as well as speak it.

A syllabary is like an alphabet, but for syllables instead of letters.) This group of marks became the Cherokee Syllabary.

It took Sequoyah a long time and a lot of hard work. People made fun of him. They called him a fool. However, in 1821, Sequoyah taught his six-year-old daughter his new system. She showed his doubting friends how it worked. Sequoyah sent his daughter far away from the house. Then the people in the house whispered a sentence. Sequoyah wrote down what they said and sent the paper to his daughter. When she called out the sentence, people were amazed. Within a few years, nearly all Cherokee could read and write their own language.

Another Cherokee hero was John Ross, who served as

In the Cherokee Syllabary each symbol represents a syllable.

chief longer than anyone. Born in 1790, he was part of the group that fought with Andrew Jackson at the Battle of Horseshoe Bend. A Cherokee saved Jackson's life in that

fight. Ross also helped transform Cherokee society. The Cherokee made laws to govern their society. John Ross was elected chief in 1827. Soon, the new leader was fighting to keep President Jackson from taking away Cherokee lands. He wrote a letter to Congress in protest. "We are stripped of every . . . freedom and . . . Our property may be plundered before our eyes . . . even our lives may be taken away . . . We have neither land nor home, nor resting place that can be called our own." Ross died in 1866 while insisting that the U.S. government honor past agreements.

John Ross helped his people adapt to growing numbers of American settlers.

The Cherokee Today

A modern Cherokee hero is Wilma Mankiller, the first woman "principal chief" of the Cherokee. Her time in

Wilma Mankiller meets President Bill Clinton after being presented the Presidential Medal of Freedom. Mankiller received the award for her leadership of the Cherokee Nation.

office lasted from 1987 to 1995. While Mankiller was chief, the Cherokee Nation tripled in size. She started health clinics for her people. One Cherokee said, "What she's done for the Cherokee Nation is nothing short of amazing." President Clinton presented Mankiller with the Medal of Freedom. He called her a ". . . leader who built a brighter and healthier future for her nation." Mankiller now advocates and raises money for many different American Indian groups.

chapter thirteen

Government

Over the years, the Cherokee have used councils, or groups of people, to solve problems and make laws.

The Cherokee Then

In earlier times, Cherokee people ruled themselves. People would gather in the town house and a town council would discuss problems. Each town looked after itself and had its own chief. There was no chief over all of the Cherokee. The law of the Cherokee was based on honor. The spoken word was most important. If a person committed a crime, his or her entire clan was responsible and had to make amends. Cherokee custom required harmony and peace among the clans.

Spring Frog was a famous Cherokee chief.

The Cherokee Today

Today, the Cherokee Nation has a fifteen-member tribal council. The Eastern Band of Cherokee Indians has a twelve-member council. The United Keetoowah Band of Cherokee Indians has nine areas, each with an elected officer. All council members are elected to make laws and improve the lives of the people.

The Cherokee Nation has a system of courts. This includes the appeals tribunal and the district court. The tribunal is the highest court of the Cherokee Nation. It hears and decides any cases where people disagree. The district court hears all cases where a tribal member has broken the laws of the Cherokee Nation. The principal chief is elected and runs the government.

This is the old Cherokee Supreme Courthouse at the Echota State Historic Site.

Moving Forward

The Cherokee Nation continues to live by its proud traditions. That includes helping land and nature by starting a clean-air project in Oklahoma.

The Cherokee have also worked hard to improve education and health care. In 1991, Chief Wilma Mankiller said, "We've managed not to just barely hang on, we've managed to move forward in a very strong . . . way."

Cherokee citizens in Oklahoma voted in 2003 to remove a section from their constitution that said that any changes to it had to be approved by the U.S. president. The United States has refused to sign it. However, the Cherokee will continue to strive for the true independence of their great nation.

Cherokee Ray McLemore and his grandson Robert "Chooch" McLemore attend a powwow that includes dancing and a basketball tournament.

Words to Know

Duyukta—This means "the right way" or "the path of being in balance."

e-du-tsi—A woman's brother who would fulfill the traditional role of uncle.

osi—Small round houses that were used during the winter months.

The Principal People—What the Cherokee often call themselves.

river cane flute—A musical instrument that is about one foot long and has five or six holes. It has a very calm and haunting sound.

shaman—Religious leader or medicine man.

syllabary—A set of symbols that represent syllables.

tear dress—A type of dress created on the Trail of Tears by using torn pieces of cloth.

town house—The building where town leaders meet.

water drum—A musical instrument that is a hollowed-out log with water inside. Deerskin is then stretched over the top.

More Books!

Birchfield, D.L. *Cherokee*. Milwaukee: Gareth Stevens Pub., 2004.

Crewe, Sabrina, and D.L. Birchfield. *The Trail of Tears*. Milwaukee: Gareth Stevens Pub., 2004.

DeAngelis, Therese. *The Cherokee: Native Basket Weavers*. Mankato, Minn.: Blue Earth Books, 2003.

Lowery, Linda. *Wilma Mankiller*. Minneapolis: Carolrhoda Books, 1996.

Rumford, James. *Sequoyah: The Man Who Gave His People Writing*. Boston, Houghton Mifflin Co., 2004.

Internet Addresses

The Cherokee Nation: Kids Corner

<http://www.cherokee.org/>

Scroll down and click on "Culture" at the left. Select "Kids' Corner" from drop-down list. Click on "Kids' Corner—Main" from new drop-down list.

History of the Cherokee

<http://cherokeehistory.com>

Index